THE
RED ARMY ★★

CELEBRATING DONS SUPPORTERS

IN ASSOCIATION WITH:

MUEHLHAN INDUSTRIAL SERVICES LTD

Muehlhan Industrial Services Ltd has been established in Aberdeen since 2007 and is part of the global Muehlhan Group, originally founded in Hamburg, Germany, in 1881. Muehlhan deliver first-class industrial services to the Oil & Gas, Marine and Renewables sectors, employing 3,000 people in 23 companies across three continents. Since becoming established in Aberdeen, Muehlhan Industrial Services Ltd has worked with local and international businesses across the UK and around the world. Muehlhan has been an active supporter of Aberdeen Football Club through sponsorship, commercial advertising and corporate events in association with the Press and Journal and Evening Express. Aberdeen FC is an integral part of the city's culture and Muehlhan is proud to offer their continued support to the team and the local community.

1983, a full Pittodrie watches Aberdeen play Dundee United.

To purchase any of the photos in this book, go to www.photoshopscotland.co.uk.

The Red Army

Celebrating Dons Supporters

By Steve Finan

ISBN 978-1-84535-803-7

First published in Great Britain in 2019 by DC Thomson & Co., Ltd.,
Meadowside, Dundee, DD1 9QJ
Copyright © DC Thomson & Co., Limited.

Visit **www.dcthomsonshop.co.uk** to purchase this book.
Or Freephone 0800 318 846 / Overseas customers call +44 1382 575580
Typeset & internal design by Steve Finan.

Body text in Times New Roman regular/**bold**/*italic* 13pt on 15 leading.

Cover design by Gary Aitchison

This book is dedicated to Bill Nicoll, Aberdonian.

INTRODUCTION

THERE are banners held up at Aberdeen FC games that bear a message familiar to all Dons fans. They read: **Soul * Spirit * Tradition**.

It is a quote from Alfredo di Stefano, manager of Real Madrid, from the famous night in 1983 when The Dons beat his team in the European Cup Winners' Cup Final. The full quote is: "Aberdeen have what money can't buy; a soul, a team spirit built in a family tradition."

Soul * Spirit * Tradition

Those three simple words capture the ethos of The Red Army.

There is a depth to the Dons' support. A loyalty and fanaticism, and a sense of humour, that sets them apart from other clubs. The support has a **soul**.

Perhaps it is the relative isolation of the city (in comparison to other Scottish football clubs) that feeds this. Perhaps it is a bond forged during those lengthy away trips. Perhaps it is an extension of the close-knit Aberdonian sense of civic pride.

Probably it is a mixture of many things. The support has **spirit**.

The Dons support is special. The Red Army travels in numbers, game after game, year after year. When the red shirts run out on any ground in any part of Scotland, the players can look round to salute a substantial and noisy band of supporters.

The League Cup Final of 2014 saw 43,000 foot soldiers of The Red Army travel to Celtic Park — the biggest single-day mass migration of football supporters in the history of Scottish football.

Aberdeen supporters rack up more miles than those of any other big club in the land. There might be a moan or two about the long trips, there might be a quine or two that doesn't enjoy waiting for her loon to return north.

But the Reds are always there, standing free. They have done this year after year, decade after decade.

The support has **tradition**.

Good times, bad times, great Dons, false dawns. They've seen them all.

George Hamilton, Bobby Clark, Joe Harper, Willie Miller, Teddy Scott, Zoltan Varga, John Hewitt . . . Leon Mike. The Red Army has shouted COYR for them all.

Soul * Spirit * Tradition

Scottish Cup Final 2017, Hampden Park.

FOREWORD

BY RICHARD GORDON

I HAVE spent countless away days in the company of Dons fans. For many years it was as a supporter bedecked in red; for the last few decades it has been with a microphone in my hand attempting to strike the on-air balance demanded by my profession.

There have inevitably been memorable moments at both ends of the enjoyment scale.

I have savoured euphoric highs while following the club that gripped my heart almost half a century ago, but I have also plumbed the depths of despair, and it was that emotion which left me in tears on my first sojourn out of the city, many years ago, with a red and white scarf wrapped around my neck.

Having won the Scottish Cup twelve months earlier, the Dons were on the verge on securing just their second League Championship title. A victory the previous week against Celtic would have all but done it, but the visitors had scrambled a draw. The final game of the season was at Falkirk and a win would keep the dream alive, so my old Dad decided we should take to the road.

Some of the details are now a bit sketchy, but we certainly crammed on to the supporters' special which left Aberdeen station on the morning of April 24th, 1971, and I clearly remember the walk along to the stadium surrounded by fellow Dons fans. There was a sense of belonging, even at such a young age, and I knew then that many such days would follow.

We lost 1-0 that day, Davie Robb conceding the penalty from which George Miller netted the only goal of the game, and Celtic went on to win the league by two points.

I cried on the way home — by no means the only time the club we all love has driven me to tears. But that was never going to dissuade me.

A few years later I was organising buses to games for my classmates at the Grammar, and after that we joined the Northern Lights Supporters Club.

For a number of seasons, I

attended virtually every away match, but it wasn't always the most comfortable of experiences.

We arrived home from Tynecastle one time without a single window in the coach, having been ambushed by Hearts fans armed with rocks; there was a similar experience at Firhill where we fled to safety across wasteland dodging bottles thrown by Thistle fans; and I recall one friend hiding under a parked car as we hastily avoided a much larger group of Dundee United fans outside Tannadice.

There were emergency stops at A&E departments around the country to drop off inebriated friends, and we even crashed off the road on one journey, the bus landing on its side in a field. But we still made it to the game in time.

Throughout all the adventures, there were those moments which made it all worthwhile.

Winning the Premier Division for the first time at Easter Road in 1980, celebrating wildly among the swaying mass of Dons fans packed

◼ *Richard doing his very best to provide balanced, non-partisan radio punditry at the 2014 Scottish League Cup Final.*

on to the terracing behind the goal; watching Willie Miller lifting aloft silverware at Hampden Park; and the biggest highlight of all, Gothenburg 1983, beating Real Madrid to win a European trophy.

There were plenty more ups and downs along the way, many of them chronicled here, and I look forward to scouring these pages to see if I can spot myself, and other familiar faces from down the years.

The Red Army is rightly acknowledged to be among the most loyal and passionate travelling supports in the country, and it is fitting that their travels and travails are being recognised in print.

Prepare to wallow in memories, good and bad, as you make your way through this excellent book.

COYR
Richard Gordon

CONTENTS

Faces In The Crowd

Some of the 36,000 Aberdeen supporters that squeezed into Pittodrie, and spread up the floodlight pylons, for a 0-0 draw with Rangers on February 20, 1971.

THIS book celebrates supporters of Aberdeen FC. Not the owners of the club, not the management, the players, or prawn sandwich-eating guests. The real fans, the weel kent faces in the crowd who go to Pittodrie and follow The Dons wherever they play.

They are tens of thousands strong. They have stood on the terraces and sat in the stands for decades. They pay their money, they make the noise, they are officially the 12th man.

They deserve to be celebrated. Loons, quines and bairns who have red and white blood and red and white hearts. They have a family tradition passed down the generations.

These people are the custodians of the club. They outlast all owners and all players and give their support in all weathers. They will be there in good times and bad.

They are the footsoldiers of The Red Army.

■ *Delighted Dons fans celebrate at Pittodrie after beating Hibs 2-1 in the last game of 2008-09, securing European football the following season.*

■ *Scottish Cup Final 1984.*

13

■ *An Ultra-special welcome for Celtic from the fans in the Richard Donald Stand on December 4, 2005. The two stars on the flag represent Aberdeen's two European trophies. No other Scottish club has won two European trophies.*

The muster of Red Army battalions at Hampden for the 2011 League Cup Semi.

2008 Scottish Cup Semi.

■ *2012 Scottish Cup Semi.*

March 22, 2014 v. Killie at Pittodrie.

■ *September 2014 v. Icy Tea at Pittodrie.*

2011 Scottish Cup Semi-Final.

2017 Scottish Cup Final.

■ *Aberdeen 4, Rangers 1. The 1982 Scottish Cup Final.*

■ *Tension. Rangers have just equalised (with a dodgy penalty) in the 1989 League Cup Final.*

■ *Couldn't get a ticket. This group had to watch the 2014 League Cup Final at The Monkey House in Union Street.*

■ *Finding themselves in a relegation battle in 1995, The Dons have just grabbed some breathing space by beating Dundee United at Pittodrie.*

■ *It took relegation play-off victories over Dunfermline to maintain Aberdeen's proud record of never having been relegated.*

Hampden Park, the Scottish Cup Semi-Final 2012. As ever, the message from the Dandies comes across loud and clear: Stand free, wherever you may be.

■ *There's nothing that is quite as satisfying as celebrating a Dons win.*

2014 — Greatest migration of fans in Scots football history

THE League Cup Final of 2014 was an incredible event. Not just for members of The Red Army, but because of a social phenomenon on a scale never before seen in Scotland.

On the day of the final, March 16, a crowd of 51,143 filed in to Celtic Park to see The Dons take on Inverness Caledonian Thistle. Around 7,000 had come from Inverness, but a magnificent and quite incredible 43,000-strong red-clad horde travelled from the Granite City.

Never before had so many people been on the move across the country in a single day.

The club had asked for even more tickets, having sold the original allocation, but health and safety fears over maintaining segregation meant the authorities refused the request.

There have been bigger crowds at cup finals, of course. But in olden days of mass attendances, a good proportion of the crowds were neutrals and hadn't travelled so far.

The Red Army was more than ready for a cup win in 2014. It had been a long 19 years since the club's last silverware.

The fans put on one of the best pre-match card displays ever seen in Scotland and the sound "sweeping in" from 43k voices was awe-inspiring. The message was clear — it was a big effort off the field, let's have a big effort on the pitch too.

It wasn't the greatest of games, to be fair. The Dons huffed and puffed, but found the Icy Tea defence hard to break down.

The 90 minutes and extra-time was goal-less. Penalties then.

The Inverness side had won their semi-final with Hearts via a penalty shoot-out so there were more than a few Dons in the ground who feared the worst and couldn't look.

But they needn't have worried. Inverness missed their first two efforts, then it eventually fell to Adam Rooney to drive the winning penalty down the middle and spark a red-and-white explosion in the stands.

The Dandy Dons were back.

The Dandies put on an incredible card display.

What an inspirational sight for the team to run out to.

It was a day when everybody

had a smile on their face.

■ *It was a day to fully enjoy with your mates.*

It was a day the young 'uns will remember all their lives.

The Red Army sang their hearts out.

■ *Those who couldn't get a ticket went to the pub and watched on TV. In McGinty's in Union Street...*

REAL ALES

LIVE SPORT

and The Stag, in Crown Street. And in just about every other alcohol-serving establishment in the toon.

■ *And when Adam Rooney tucked away the deciding penalty, the on-field Reds ran to celebrate with the off-field Reds. We've won the cup.*

WE BELIEVED

hat money can't buy -

The next game was Kilmarnock at home. The Red Army showed their appreciation of the team.

An Aberdeen tradition

THE Aberdeen support might not have always called themselves The Red Army (such nicknames are fairly modern) but they have always been legion. Aberdeen FC is traditionally a very well-supported club. If there is a good team on the park, then Dons fans will turn out in huge numbers. That is true today, just as it was true 50 years ago, just as it was true 100 years ago. The people of Aberdeen have always been greatly proud of their football club.

■ *September 27, 1958 — a healthy crowd turned out at Pittodrie to see a sparkling display, an excellent 3-1 win over Celtic. Young outside-left George Mulhall was the star of the day.*

4

Association.

ABERDEEN A STEP NEARER SCOTTISH CUP.

To Meet Hamilton, Hearts, or Rangers in Semi-Final.

OVER 40,000 SEE CELTIC "BOGEY" LAID AT PITTODRIE.

By "Clansman."

Aberdeen, Hamilton, Hearts, and Rangers have qualified for the semi-final of the Scottish Cup, and Wednesday's draw will be awaited with the keenest interest by northern sportsmen.

Aberdeen's was a magnificent victory. They laid the Celtic "bogey" in no uncertain fashion, and finished worthy winners of a desperate encounter. "Matt" Armstrong got two goals from the penalty spot, while Mills headed a brilliant third counter. The official attendance was 40,105, which broke all records for the ground.

The biggest surprise of the round was the margin of Rangers' win at Fir Park. The Light Blues scored four times to Motherwell's once. Smith was the hero of the match, the big centre netting all four goals for the winners.

For weeks on end Rangers have been

■ Left: One of the all-time great Scottish football photos from between the wars. The date is March 9th, 1935, the queue down the Merkland Road to get in to the Scottish Cup Quarter-Final against Celtic.

■ Right, the view of that game from inside the ground. The official attendance was 40,105, although there would have been hundreds, possibly thousands, more youngsters lifted over the turnstiles.

■ Above, the P&J report on the game

■ *A true Aberdonian must be an Aberdeen FC supporter. The two pictures here show the legacy of the club.*

You are a Don, following in the footsteps of your father — who followed in the footsteps of his father. Your children will be Aberdeen supporters, and their children after them.

Support your home town club.

If you're an Aberdonian, then you follow The Reds. It cannot feel right or be right to support another club from another city, or another country.

When The Dons win, the whole city celebrates. If The Dons lose, then the city mourns as one.

Aberdeen is a Red city. The population are Reds.

■ *Left, a famous day for any Aberdeen supporter — August 17th, 1946. The score was Aberdeen 6, Celtic 2.*

The photo has spent a long time in an archive folder and is showing signs of its age.

■ *Almost 42,000 packed Pittodrie for the 1953 Scottish Cup Quarter-Final replay between The Dons and Hibernian. Any vantage point was quickly snapped up, while many more disappointed fans were locked out. Aberdeen won 2-0.*

■ *Another famous old Aberdeen FC photo. August 13, 1947, a midweek game against Hibs. The ground was so full that spectators overflowed on to the roof of the enclosure and were several deep on the cinder track . . .*

. . . resulting in a scene, and
a fan's eyeview of the game,
that it just isn't possible to
experience these days.

■ *An early shot of The Red Army on manoeuvres. Aberdeen supporters at Joint Station on April 24th, 1954, awaiting the special to Glasgow for the Cup Final against Celtic.*

■ *And a section of the crowd at the '54 final.*

■ The greatest crowd of all. The incredible attendance of 147,365 at the Aberdeen v. Celtic Scottish Cup Final on April 24th, 1937, is a European record for a club game. It is a record that will never now be beaten.

Picture shows Dons centre-half George Thomson and Celtic's Jimmy McGrory chasing a loose ball. Dons keeper George Johnstone lies spread-eagled, with full-back Willie Cooper running in behind him.

In the background the North Terracing of Hampden seethes with crammed-in supporters.

The 1960s

THE first half of the 1960s was a relatively difficult time for Dons fans. The manager was Tommy Pearson, whose "double-shuffle" had made him a great favourite with the Pittodrie crowd when he had played at inside-left for The Dons. But his six-year spell as manager, 1959-65, didn't match his own stellar standards of entertainment.

It changed when Eddie Turnbull, one of the stars of Hibs' Famous Five forward line, was brought in from his job as coach of Queen's Park. The Red Army loved him.

He was a pugnacious, determined character and refused to accept second best. He led the red legions on some wonderful adventures in his six-year reign, the highlight being the 1970 Scottish Cup win.

But he was also the architect of the fantastic run to the 1967 Cup Final, which included one of those incredible nights when football fever really grips the city.

The quarter-final replay with Hibs on Wednesday, March 22nd, had the fans in a frenzy. The teams had drawn 1-1 at Easter Road but The Dons turned in a sizzling performance to win the second game 3-0.

What a night — one of The Red Army's finest hours up to that point. A crowd of 44,000 squeezed in to Pittodrie and the place boiled with enthusiasm and partisan backing for the boys on the park .

None who were there will ever forget it.

It was the precursor to many more great nights under the lights that would come in later years.

These pages, and the previous two pages show scenes from that incredible night in March 1967.

There has always been a special feel about Pittodrie for big midweek games.

Emotions ran particularly high for this game. Every voice seemed louder, the sways of the crowd added to the excitement, there was a buzz and enthusiasm that was almost palpable.

The experience of watching the game of football changed in the 1960s, not just in Aberdeen but up and down the UK. The previous gentlemanly Corinthian spirit was replaced by a more partisan, fiercely tribal atmosphere. Songs became louder, celebrations became wilder.

It was a heady, addictive time to be attending football matches.

■ *February 23rd, 1966. A pitch invasion to congratulate the team on demolishing Dundee United 5-0 in a Scottish Cup second round tie.*

■ *The queues to get in (left-hand page) and the crowd inside Pittodrie for a hard-fought 1-1 draw with Celtic on Christmas Eve, 1966.*

Red and proud in the 1970s

THE 1970s was a transitional time for Aberdeen FC and The Red Army. The decade saw some good managers, the emergence of great players, a growing realisation of the club's place in Scottish football, and the beginning of that fiery ambition that would elevate Aberdeen above all other clubs to become the pre-eminent challengers to the Old Firm.

The Red Army turned out in numbers during all of this, and the footsoldiers of those days are the parents and grandparents of the Pittodrie support of today.

You are a Red because they were Reds. You should thank them for that.

In this chapter, you will see the older supporter, who still goes to matches, in their younger days. There is an honour to be had if you spot yourself or a relative on these pages because these are the fans who played a part in building Aberdeen up to become the great side of the 1980s and the modern, highly professional and success-hungry outfit it is today.

■ *Young Dons show the flag before joining the cup-tie special at Aberdeen Joint Station. The date was Saturday, March 6th, 1971, a Scottish Cup Quarter-Final away to Rangers.*

■ *The 1970s started with a bang. Aberdeen won the Cup with the now legendary Derek "Cup-Tie" McKay scoring his only four goals for Aberdeen — the winners in the quarter and semi-finals and two in the final itself. These supporters are off to the quarter-final at Falkirk, on February 21st, 1970.*

ABERDEEN FC

■ *March 14th,
1970. Fans at the
station on their
way to Muirton
Park, Perth, for the
semi-final against
Kilmarnock.*

■ *Amidst a sea of celebrations at Hampden, captain Martin Buchan lifts the 1970 Scottish Cup after the 3-1 victory over Celtic.*

Celtic, who would play in the European Cup Final a few weeks later, had been hot favourites to complete a domestic treble.

But Cup-Tie McKay and a Joe Harper penalty put paid to that.

There was a tremendous Dons travelling support at Hampden that day, and a fabulous welcome (see page 242) when the lads returned north with the trophy.

■ *The Cup Quarter-Final against Motherwell at Pittodrie on March 8th, 1975, was another of those matches that gripped the imagination of the whole town.*

The game went down in Red Army folklore as one of the most one-sided games ever seen at Pittodrie. Before a 23,400 crowd Aberdeen outclassed 'Well in all departments and created chance after chance. Motherwell had one attack and won 1-0.

■ *October 1st, 1975. The Anglo-Scottish Cup Quarter-Final against Middlesbrough. The competition was taken seriously at the time and drew a 9,000 crowd.*

■ *November 2nd, 1976. These were good times at Pittodrie.*

A crowd of more than 15,000 saw The Dons beat Motherwell 3-1 to go top of the league, and Ally MacLeod's boys were to contest the League Cup Final four days later.

PRIZE DRAW
20 FRIDGES FILLED WIT...

20 FRIDGES FILLED with FOOD

20 FRIDGES FILLED with FOOD

Ally MacLe...
MANAGER, ABERDEEN F.C. CUP-WINNE...
WILL MAKE THE DRA...
on THURSDAY 2nd DECEMB...
at 6·30 p.m.

20 FRIDGES FILLED with FOOD

NORCO HOUSE

NORCO HOUSE

20 FRIDGES FILLE...

20 FRIDGES FILLER...

■ *The charismatic, and often underestimated, Super Ally was only at Pittodrie for 18 months, but won the League Cup and realigned the club's ambitions. He laid the foundations for further success. In this 1976 photo he is picking winners for a Norco House fridge competition.*

*November 6th, 1976.
A Red Army squad from
Mastrick off to Hampden.*

■ *September 1977. Rosehill House. Businessman and lifelong Red George Geddes pushes forward plans to form a new branch of the Aberdeen FC Supporters Club, to be known as the Northern Lights.*

■ *September 17th, 1977. The start of the shift in power. Dons fans watching Billy McNeill's charges beat Celtic 2-1.*

Aberdeen were top of the Premier Division with nine points after five games. Celtic were equal bottom with Clydebank, on one point.

■ *Dons fans at the Cowdray Hall before setting off for the 1978 Scottish Cup Final.*

■ *The 1978 Final. A scruffy old photo, but the author's favourite in the entire book. Flares and long hair. This is what football was like in the 1970s. Violence hadn't yet been "organised", the terraces swayed as the game ebbed and flowed, and the chants were stupidly childish. It was all great fun.*

■ *The Red Army headed to Hampden for the 1978 Final, colourful and noisy as away trips usually are.*

This raucous group, some with carrier bags full of sandwiches and cans of fizzy pop (possibly), travelled from Aberdeen Joint Station on one of the special trains that were run.

It was a 2-1 defeat on the day, and this would be Billy McNeill's last game in charge. An up-and-coming young manager was on his way to Pittodrie from St Mirren.

The fortunes of The Red Army were soon to change, and Scottish football history was about to be made.

ENTRANCE TO PLATFORMS
6 NORTH END
7 AND 8

■ *Two shots of The Red Army crammed into Dens Park for a League Cup Semi-Final win over Hibs on December 13th, 1978.*

The thousands who had made their way down the road for the game were rewarded by Stuart Kennedy's extra-time winner.

■ *Three shots of fans on the way to the League Cup Final of March 31st, 1979 — leaving from the train and bus stations. The match is memorable for Doug Rougvie's ridiculous sending off. But then, who among The Red Army was surprised by a dodgy decision when playing one of the Old Firm in Glasgow?*

■ *There were two League Cup Finals in 1979 spanning two seasons. This is the Pittodrie crowd celebrating Aberdeen's progression towards the second of those finals with a 3-2 Quarter-Final First-Leg win over Celtic on October 31st.*

■ *On to the League Cup Semi against Morton at the neutral venue of Hampden . . . 24 miles from Cappielow and just the 150 miles from Pittodrie.*

IAN SCANLON SWIVELS QUICKER THAN A PARKER-KNOLL

■ *Morton were seen off 2-1 and The Red Army was set for another cup final.*

■ *December 8th, 1979. Red Army members about to board a special at Joint Station on the way to Hampden for the League Cup Final.*

■ *This was long before card displays were thought of, but the Dons supporters turned out in droves for that final and put on a highly impressive flag-waving display in the covered end of Hampden.*

■ *On to the replay at a cold and wet Dens Park and The Red Army faithfully attended again in impressive numbers. Wherever the team play, they are there.*

They come fae a ooer

ABERDEEN Football Club represents the city, but is also recognised as "the team" for Aberdeenshire, the north of Scotland, and even further afield. The lure of The Reds knows no borders.

There is an evident pride displayed in banners attaching the names of surrounding towns and villages to the Red cause.

This tradition of a widely dispersed support is a long-standing one and these far-flung regiments are always welcomed into The Red Army.

■ *Below — 1992. Young strikers Colin Milne and Eoin Jess visit the Orkney branch of the Supporters' Club.*

■ *Young fans from Gairloch, Wester Ross, visit Pittodrie in March 1982.*

■ *1983. Adding that second star. Some of Golspie's Dons supporters who were at Pittodrie for the Aberdeen-Hamburg European Super Cup Final Second Leg.*

■ 1984. Members of the 120-strong Inverness branch of the Supporters' Association display their new banner.

2008. Crieff Dons reminded Bayern Munich fans of a feared name from the past: "Aberdeen FC". One of the Germans could bear-ly look!

■ *Inverurie and Stonehaven colours fly as The Red Army occupies Fola Esch, Luxembourg, in 2016.*

1993. The Newton Stewart Supporters Club visit Pittodrie. The town is in Dumfries & Galloway, a 450-mile round trip for the 36 club members.

The boys from The Broch set off for Gothenburg '83.

And many a sight I've seen

WHENEVER The Dons play in Scotland, they take a fantastic travelling support with them. The Red Army travels in numbers that are frankly quite astonishing.

The lengthy treks take hours (especially the bottleneck coming through Dundee) by bus. That doesn't put them off.

The hostile reception at some grounds is often downright nasty. That doesn't put them off.

The weather can be a real pain, especially at some of the older, leakier Scottish football grounds. And the bus parks are often a long, rain-battered trudge away. That doesn't put them off.

Travelling all those miles can cost an absolute fortune. Even that doesn't put them off.

Wherever The Dons go, The Red Army invasion is close behind. They bring colour, noise and atmosphere.

No other team in Scotland takes such a huge proportion of their support with them so consistently. If you measure it by calculating travelling supporter per head of city population, then Aberdeen have the best away support in the nation.

And that has been a plain truth for season after season, decade after decade. Stand Free and be proud of that.

Unhappy faces at Tynecastle in 2003.

Scottish Cup shenanigans at Arbroath in January 2005.

RED ULTRAS

RED ULTR

■ *Tannadice again (where they clearly can't spell) in 2005.*

■ *May 2015 — showing Dundee United what a flag display should look like.*

■ *The longest away day of all. It is 211.3 miles from Pittodrie to Queen of the South's Palmerston Park. That's further than the trip from Manchester United to Chelsea. But the Red Army faithfully travelled in big numbers for this Tuesday night Scottish Cup replay on St Valentine's Day 2012.*

■ *Wigged up and on the way to Hampden for the Scottish Cup Semi-Final, 2011.*

Hibs away. Scottish Cup 2007.

■ *Celebrations at Fir Park, Motherwell, in August 2013.*

Fir Park again, a Scottish Cup Quarter-Final in 2012. No fans do away-from-home card displays quite as well as The Red Army.

■ *May 1995. The Dons should never have found themselves in a relegation play-off. However, beating Dunfermline was celebrated long and hard. Photos from the away leg at East End Park.*

Kilmarnock, February 2008. You can tell by the faces that the game isn't going well.

■ *Dens Park, October 2014. Dandies celebrate The Dons giving Dundee FC their customary thrashing.*

■ Ibrox is the biggest away fixture. These pictures are from 2012 and 2009. The Rangers fans would have seen the funny side of the banner on the left. Probably. You've got to have a sense of humour — see also page 290.

■ *The Scottish League released a statement praising the behaviour of both sets of fans after the 1995 League Cup Final between The Dons and Dundee at Hampden.*

The League's assistant secretary of the time, David Thomson, said, "Both sets of supporters were very well behaved. It would be great if every final had a similar family atmosphere."

In reality, the main reason the game had such an atmosphere was that The Red Army knew the team was going to win. There was a feeling of confidence running through the supporters and players — and Aberdeen did win it, with ease. It was only 2-0, but the result was never in danger.

Still, it was nice of the League chap to say kind words for a change, recognising that not all football supporters are knuckle-dragging thugs.

Pittodrie

THE old place has seen some high times over the years. And like any grand old lady, she still has class and character, and retains a formidable presence.

The day is coming when The Red Army will no longer troop the colours at Pittodrie. The move to a new ground is progress, of course, a forward-looking club has to move with the times. The relocation will be exciting in itself, but Pittodrie will for ever have a hold on the red hearts of Aberdeen fans.

There are memories invested in the place that can never die.

ABERDEEN FOOTBALL CLUB LTD

5/-

■ *Pittodrie 1969. It's an Aberdeen landmark. You go there, as did your father and grandfather.*

■ *It can be a bit nippy.
This blizzard forced the Dons-
St Johnstone game of January
3rd, 1984, to be abandoned at
half-time, and caused power
cuts across Aberdeenshire.
Goodness knows how the
crowd made it home that day.*

■ *Sharp-dressed Mods in the summer of 1967, or millennials in the hard winter of 2010 . . . they all go to Pittodrie.*

CONDOR SLICED
A GALLAHER TOBACCO
ALES AND STOUT
BLACK VELVET PORT
SERVICE

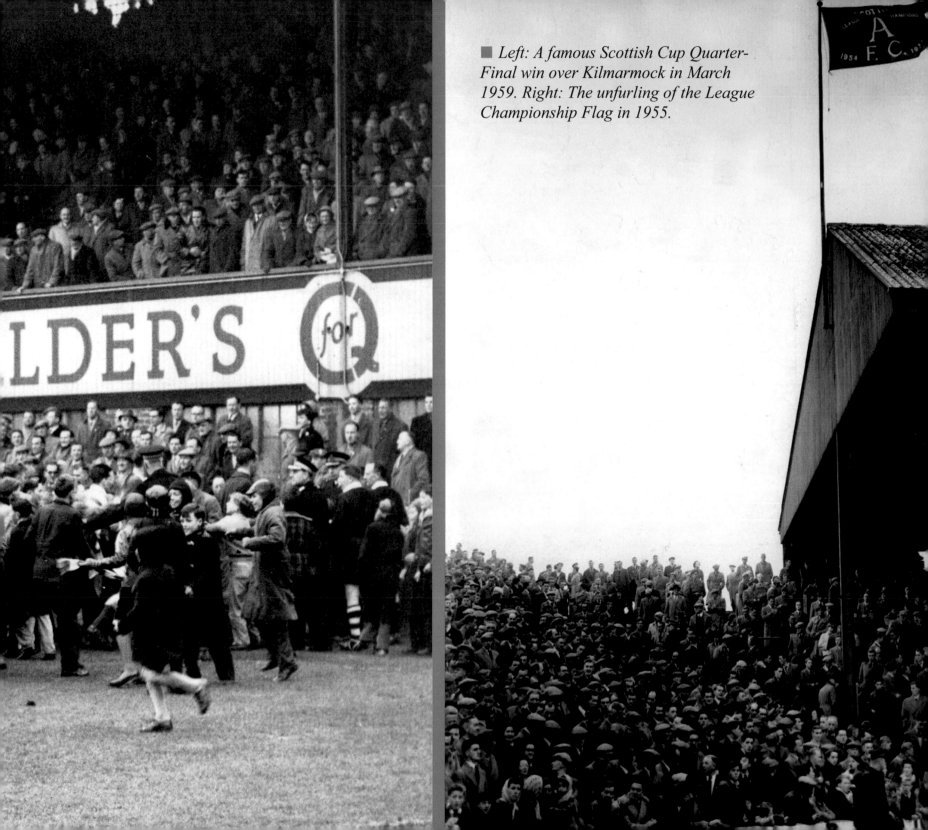

■ *Left: A famous Scottish Cup Quarter-Final win over Kilmarnock in March 1959. Right: The unfurling of the League Championship Flag in 1955.*

■ *There's nothing quite like a European night under the lights. Even Sleepy Hollow rattles the pan drops more vigorously. This is Aberdeen v. Bayern Munich, UEFA Cup, February 14th, 2008.*

144   RED ARMY

■ *Pittodrie, and its surrounds, have changed over the years. Whether you preferred the old or the new is up to you. Left: an aerial view from 1952. This page: The Beach End, 1973.*

146 RED ARMY

September 7th, 1929. Aberdeen 1, Rangers 1.
Crowd: 32,600.

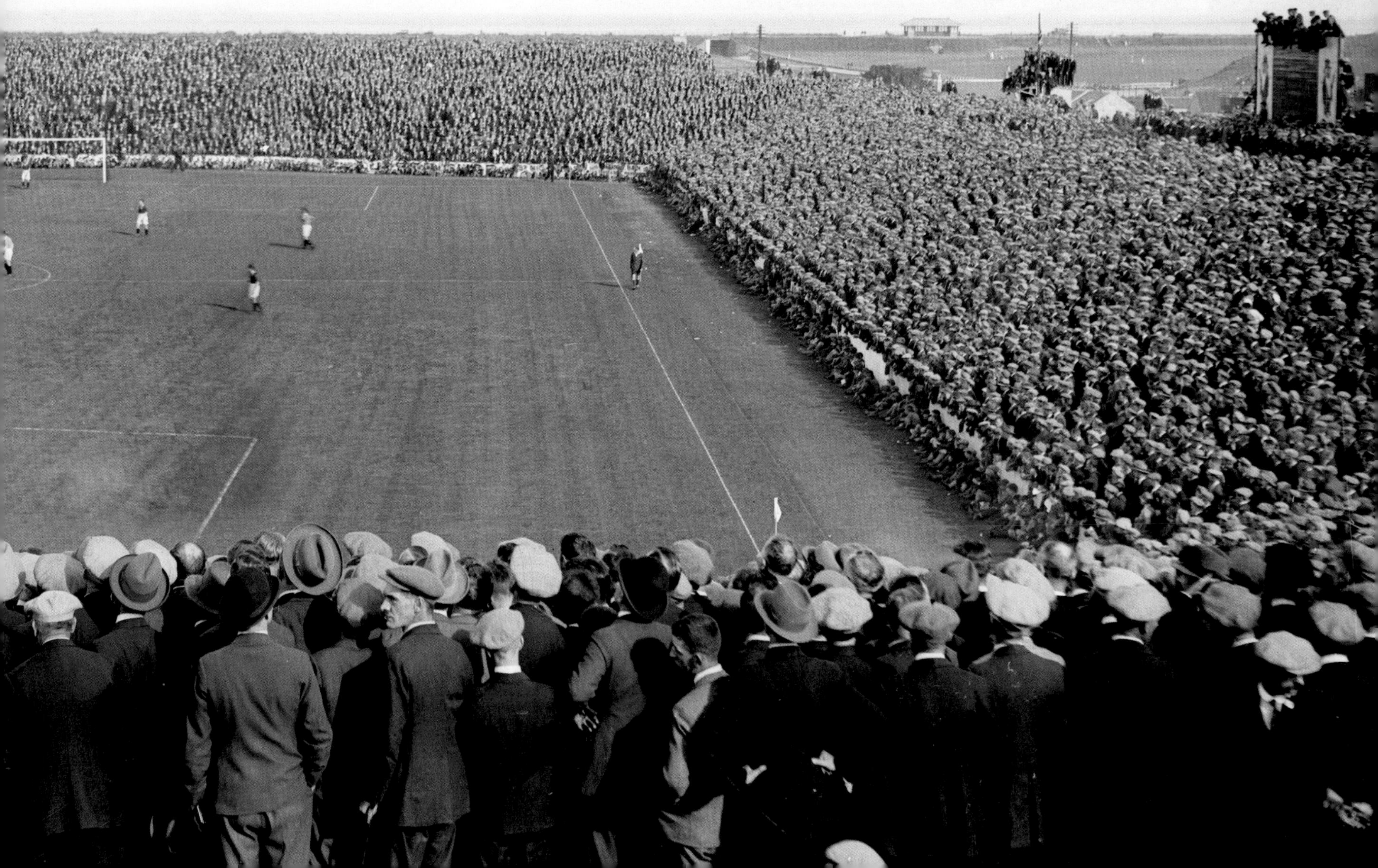

■ *A view of Pittodrie in April 1982, during a 3-1 Premier Division win over Rangers.*

■ *Dons of a new era. The Richard Donald stand was first used for a competetive fixture on Tuesday, August 11th, 1993, a 5-0 rout of Clydebank.*

■ *Another "new" stand. The old Paddock officially became the Merkland Stand in 1985. The first time it was fully opened was for a League Cup Semi-Final second leg 1-0 win over Dundee United, on Wednesday, October 9th.*

■ *Sorry, you'll have had to turn your book on its side. It is September 1989 and this photo shows the down side of the outdoor sport that is football. Sometimes, when it rains — it really rains.*

■ *When the club finally leaves Pittodrie it will leave behind a part of itself. Pittodrie was, and is, a great stadium. It oozes character from every girder. It may have been a bit cold at times. It may also have had a "too quiet" reputation as the crowd sat back and waited to be impressed. But it was also a tough away fixture for any team, and when full and "up" for a big game it played a part in the victories.*

■ *Whatever the new ground at Kingsford is like, it will be jointly the team's and The Red Army's responsibility to create a new fortress in the north.*

Fergie-time

ALEX FERGUSON wasn't created a "Sir" during his time at Aberdeen, but it could be argued that the most noteworthy achievements of his career were made during his time in the North.

He didn't just challenge the Old Firm, he dominated them. He didn't just make Aberdeen good, he made them formidable. He didn't just craft The Dons into a winning side, he made them serial winners feared by every club across the continent.

He gathered 10 major trophies in seven years. The pinnacle was Gothenburg of course (see page 174) but there were many more highs.

The Red Army loved their Fergie-time. They fully supported what the great man was doing. They filled Pittodrie, making it a hugely difficult place for other teams to come to, and travelled to away games in record-breaking numbers.

The team on the pitch was top class, so was the support off the pitch.

■ *April 12th, 1980. An estimated 10,000 Aberdeen supporters flocked to Hampden for the Scottish Cup Semi-Final against Rangers.*

■ *Wednesday, May 7th, 1980. The Red Army knew the Championship had been secured the previous Saturday, with a five-goal thrashing of Hibs. The Dons would have had to concede 10 goals at Partick Thistle to lose the title on goal-difference. That was never going to happen. A 1-1 draw confirmed Fergie's first title and The Red Army went mental in Maryhill.*

■ *October 22nd, 1980. Aberdeen's European Cup campaign featured a tie with the most glamorous side on the continent at the time, Liverpool, with the first leg at Pittodrie.*

■ *November 5th, 1980. Around 3,000 members of The Red Army headed south to Anfield for the second leg.*

■ *September 30th , 1981. Fergie's Dons welcomed Bobby Robson's Ipswich to Pittodrie for a UEFA Cup tie . . . and destroyed them.*

■ *The best night of all. The ECWC Quarter-Final, March 16th, 1983. Fergie's Reds beat Bayern Munich 3-2, after twice being behind. One of the best games The Red Army has ever seen at Pittodrie.*

The second half of Fergie's 1983 double. The Dons beat Rangers at Hampden to win The Scottish Cup.

■ COYR, shouted
Wee Alickie on
the front page of
The Express.

165

The ECWC Semi-Final First Leg — April 6th, 1983. The Dons battered Belgians Waterschei Thor 5-1 at Pittodrie.

■ *Here we go, here we go! May 19th, 1984. Dons fans wait for their train at Aberdeen Station, on the way to lifting that year's Scottish Cup. Victory over Celtic in Glasgow was no surprise to anyone.*

■ *A section of the thousands who turned up at Pittodrie to greet their heroes and celebrate the 1984 League and Cup double. The Reds were given a 20-minute standing ovation — recognition of one of the all-time great Scottish club sides.*

■ *Fergie's teams did things like this with seeming ease. They were 2-0 down after the first leg of the 1984 ECWC Quarter-Final to Újpest Dozsa, but stormed to a 3-0 victory in the second leg as if it were their divine right to do such things. What a team they were. What times they gave The Red Army.*

■ *A Red Army Brigade about to board a football special bound for the 1986 Scottish Cup Final, a 3-0 trouncing of Hearts. Easy!*

JIM LEIGHTON MORE CLEAN SHEETS THAN DAZ!

■ *The 1985 Skol Cup Final at Hampden. The Red Army salute their heroes as Fergie's Dons whup Hibs 3-0.*

■ *The man himself waving the 1980 Premier Division trophy.*

Sir Alexander Chapman Ferguson brought unprecedented glory to Aberdeen FC and he is rightly revered by The Red Army.

As long as the game is played or remembered in Scotland his name will stand as the prime example of how to recruit, man-manage, and set up a winning football team.

Gothenburg, the Red invasion

THE Red Army invaded the Swedish city in numbers that are mind-boggling. Sixty planes were chartered, the P&O Ferry *St Clair* set sail (see page 192) and various other crazy and convoluted routes were found. There were around 12,000 Aberdonians there that night, outnumbering the Real Madrid fans by at least four to one.

The days before the final were tense yet great fun in the city, as fans partied with the Swedes and every loon and quine took a wander past the bank window where the European Cup-Winners' Cup trophy was displayed.

The game itself was the career highlight of those players wearing the shirts, but the wild celebrations in the deluge-soaked stands were the property of The Red Army.

There never was a feeling such as the one that spread through the ranks of red as Willie Miller, with his familiar one-handed, open armed grasp of the cup, saluted those who felt the most about this victory.

The quote is given in the introduction to this book, but deserves to be repeated here. Alfredo di Stefano said: "Aberdeen have what money can't buy; a soul, a team spirit built in a family tradition."

He was talking about the team. But he captured the essence of the fans.

■ *It was wet, but it was wonderful.*

■ *This was where everyone was heading, the Ullevi Stadium, Gothenburg.*

■ *Even those who couldn't travel turned out to wish the lads all the best — this was Greenbrae Primary's special cheer.*

■ *The District Council ran a draw to fly 33 special ambassador schoolchildren out to the game.*

■ *There were many ways to get to Sweden. This group (left) gathered at the Cowdray Hall for a long, long coach trip to Gothenburg.*

■ *Right: three generations of the Tait family from Cairnbulg, up near Fraserburgh, took a plane. Standing, from left, Mrs Kathleen Tait and daughters Lisa (7) and Michelle (12), alongside fisherman Billy Tait and son Thomas (14). Front (kneeling) Peter Tait (15) and his cousin, Martin West. Missing from the photo is grandfather Peter Tait, who was checking in for the flight.*

■ *Inverness and Elgin-based fans set off from Inverness Airport.*

The Red Army made noise and friends in Sweden's second largest city. The stage was set.

■ *And when The Dons took to the field to be greeted by the massed ranks of The Red Army . . . they couldn't lose.*

■ Left. The weather didn't help — any member of The Red Army who was there will tell you they got somewhat damp!

■ But the weel kent faces (above) just got out the brollies and got on with it. It was a European Final, after all.

■ Right: Never mind the weather. We all know what happened. No supporter who was there or who watched on TV will ever forget what it felt like to see Willie hoist that trophy. Those were the days of your lives. It was an incredible achievement and a wonderful performance by players and fans alike. Look at Gordon Strachan, he can barely believe what he has just been a part of. No Scottish team has won a European trophy since Aberdeen did it (twice) in 1983. COYR.

■ *Then it was home to a wild reception from an adoring city, and beyond. The pupils of Auchterless Primary were given permission to forget school uniform for the day and wear the red and white.*

DONS ARE ACE

DONS, WE ♥ U

■ *Albyn School, then an all-girls establishment, reckoned the victorious Dons were "ace".*

■ *Fergie led the team on the traditional open-topped bus victory parade.*

■ *It was one of the stand-out days in the long and proud history of the city of Aberdeen.*

Voyage of The Red Navy

THE *M.V. St Clair* deserves a chapter of her own. The Red Navy set sail for Gothenburg '83 on the boat that rocked. The P&O ferry, which usually plied the Aberdeen-Shetland route, was chartered as the world's first floating football special.

Alex Ferguson himself was at dockside to see the ship off on the Monday before the final and would be there, with a hung-over Mark McGhee and the European Cup Winners' Cup trophy, to welcome her back to Aberdeen.

The journey was quite something. There were 493 fans aboard, and almost 25,000 cans of beer.

There were cabins and recliner chairs to relax upon, but there was also one of the great achievements of Scottish football history to be celebrated and sung about.

There had never been anything quite like it before, and never has been since. The voyage of the Red Navy has passed into Aberdeen FC legend.

■ *Hundreds were on board, while hundreds more gathered to see the St Clair off at the dock.*

■ *Alex Ferguson himself waved them on their way.*

■ *And off they went to sail the seas.*

The view from the boat as she left.

■ *Those on board whiled away the journey with philosophical discussions and other gentlemanly pursuits.*

Fergie and Mark McGhee, with the trophy, welcomed the boat back. It was an 18-hour trip each way, but will last a lifetime in the memory of all those who saw service with The Red Navy aboard the St Clair.

You need a ticket

IF you want to see The Dons you've got to get a ticket. And if you want a ticket, sometimes you'll have to queue up for it.

Throughout the club's history, big games have come along with regularity. Sometimes Pittodrie wasn't big enough or the allocation for an away game was low.

True fans, the week-in week-out regulars, accept this. They know that the fairweather supporters will always come out for the "biggies". So they get up early, stand in line, do whatever it takes get their hands on a ticket.

It's the only way . . . after all, you can't miss a big game, can you.

201

March 1985. Members of The Red Army wait patiently in line for Scottish Cup Quarter-Final tickets.

The Dons (holders) played Rangers in a Scottish Cup Quarter-Final at Ibrox in March 1971. The queue for tickets stretched round the Merkland Road end.

■ *There were often queues to see Fergie's incredible Dons team. This was Pittodrie under siege when tickets for the 1981 UEFA cup-tie against trophy holders Ipswich Town went on sale. Holders or not, The Dons saw them off fairly easily, 3-1.*

204 RED ARMY

■ *Pittodrie Street can be an affy cauld place when the winter winds blow up it. Most of those near the front of this queue, for a League game against Rangers in November 1978, had been in place all night.*

February 1979. More freezing dedication — another all-nighter for tickets to see Aberdeen v. Celtic. In the end, the cold weather forced a postponement of the game.

LEAGUE CUP FINAL

TICKETS

SOLD HERE

■ *Start them young. Eight-year-old Mark Chalmers, Bridge of Don, waited a long time to get his tickets for the March 1979 League Cup Final.*

■ *April 1980. Three-year-old Lynne Alexander, of Kittybrewster, got tickets for herself and her mates for an ASC awayday trip down the road to Tannadice.*

208   RED ARMY

■ Sometimes it was different. It was a queue for that most desperate of scenarios for a supporter — the wait to get into a game that had already started, and the police and stewards were deciding whether to let more inside. It just doesn't happen in these more regulated modern times. Younger supporters will never have had to suffer this.

It was agony. You could hear the crowd inside, hear the chants, you wondered what the howls of outrage and rounds of applause were signifying. You could "feel" the game, but couldn't see it.

It is an experience that managers, players and journalists (in their pampered, heated box in the stand, with free half-time nibbles) never understood.

But if you were 10 minutes late, or stayed in the pub for one half-pint too many, this was what could happen. It didn't matter if you were a regular every other week, and felt deep in your heart that you truly deserved to get into this game. None of that counted. You just had to hope that the "match commander" policeman would find it in his heart to squeeze a few more punters through the turnstiles.

This was a Scottish Cup Quarter-Final replay with Hearts in March 1985. The Dons won 1-0.

STAND

STAND
TICKETS 'Q' HERE →

5

■ *Flares and fanaticism. Part of the long queue for 1978 Cup Final tickets.*

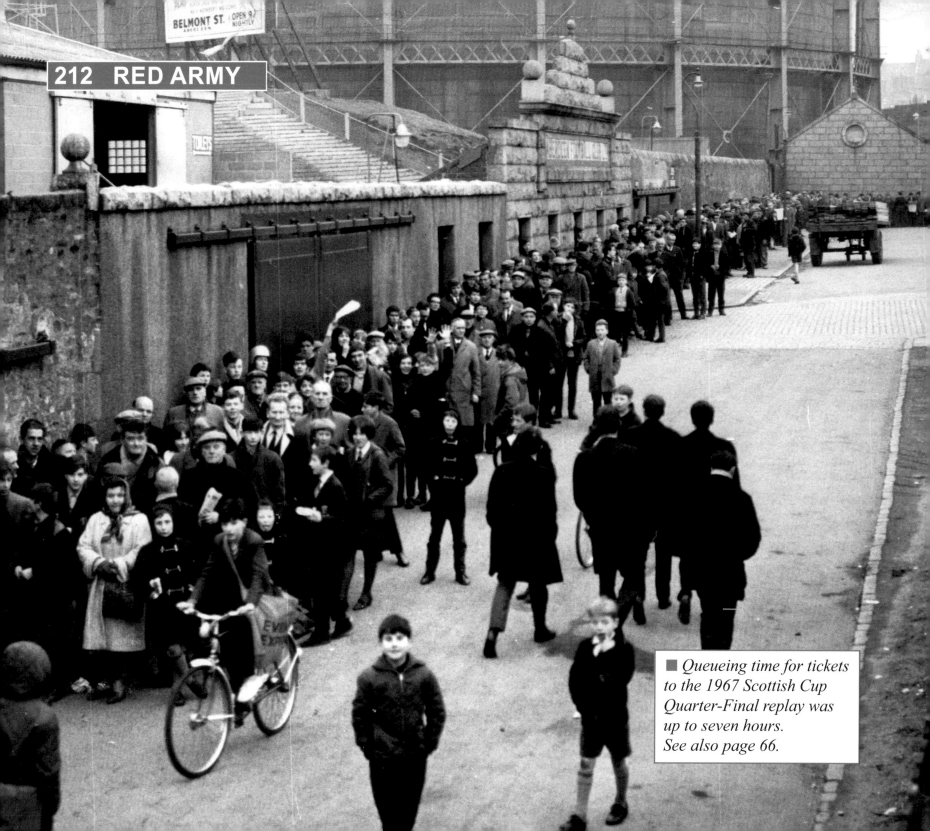

Queueing time for tickets to the 1967 Scottish Cup Quarter-Final replay was up to seven hours. See also page 66.

■ *This last "queue" photo serves as proof of what makes Dons fans just a little bit different. This isn't for a cup final or crunch Euro tie, it is the line for Dons legend Bobby Clark's testimonial in 1978. The fans started arriving at 2am for their chance to pay tribute to a hero. The Aberdeen first team played a Former Dons Select in front of 21,000 true Reds.*

CENTRE STAND
SEASON TICKETS BCD

ALL CHILDREN MUST PAY FULL PRICE

SPECTATORS CARRYING CANS, BOTTLES OR MISSILES WILL NOT BE ADMITTED

Euro adventures

A N overseas trip to see your team play is one of the best adventures you can have with your mates. It's a kaleidoscope of new experiences, and it's even better if you travel with reasonable confidence that your team is going to do well.

The Red Army invaded Europe on many memorable occasions as the club wrote its name into the history of the Continent's football competitions, from Iceland to Kazakhstan.

■ *Below — 1980. Tom McKenzie snapped up 54 tickets for the European Cup second-leg clash between Liverpool and Aberdeen at Anfield on behalf of fans from Mugiemoss Recreation Club, where he was steward.*

On tour in Germany. The Northern Lights Supporters Club about to board a bus for a lengthy trip to Eintracht Frankfurt in October 1979.

JOE HARPER STRIKES FASTER THAN "SCOTTISHBLUEBELL"

The crate of tins is for medicinal purposes.

On tour in Latvia. FK Ventspils, July 2016.

On tour in Spain.
Real Sociedad, July 2014.

On tour in Ireland.
St Patrick's Athletic, June 2014.

On tour in the Czech Republic.
Sigma Olomouc, August 2009.

■ *On tour in Italy.*
Two Torino photos,
October 1993.

■ *On tour in Slovenia.*
NK Maribor, August 2016.

■ *The greatest Euro trip of them all — Gothenburg '83. But that is a longer tale. See pages 174 and 192.*

The Red Army is a family

T HERE is a long and proud tradition of the Aberdeen FC-supporting community looking after their own. A passed-on soldier of The Red Army remains a hero for ever.

There can be no solace when a loved one leaves us, but recognition and shared grieving can serve a purpose for the bereaved. It can be good to know you're not alone. To have the ranks of The Red Army standing shoulder-to-shoulder by you in a time of trouble is no small thing.

But it isn't all bad times. The Red Army has happy times, times to celebrate, and things to smile about that aren't to do with what is happening on the pitch.

■ *Teddy Scott was one of the club's great heroes. He filled almost every coaching role at the club over the course of 50 years and was a friend and mentor to young players coming through. Any supporter who went on a Pittodrie tour would speak fondly of meeting Teddy and the warm welcome he gave. Teddy died in 2012, aged 83, and The Red Army paid tribute to him. Rest in peace Teddy.*

■ *In 2016 members of The Red Army left tributes to superfan Norman Goldie who died aged 87. The club retired his seat in the Merkland Stand and painted it half red-half white, in honour of Norman's footwear. He famously walked to every home game in sandals and mismatched red and white socks. Rest in peace Norman.*

■ James Stewart was just 16 when he died of osteosarcoma, a form of bone cancer. The Red Army paid a touching tribute to one of their own at the match against Hamilton on Sunday, April 3rd, 2016. His name will live for ever. Rest in peace James.

■ *Lifelong Red Army member Michael McCartney died of a brain tumour in 2016. He was 51. On his bucket list had been to watch a match, with friends and family, from the comfort of a box seat. He was joined by Joe Harper, the man whose goals first made Michael fall under the spell of The Dons. Rest in peace Michael.*

■ *The Red Army unveiled a tribute to former player Graham Leggat, a member of the glorious Championship-winning side of 1954-55 and the League Cup-winning team of 1955-56. Graham died in 2015, aged 81. Rest in peace Graham.*

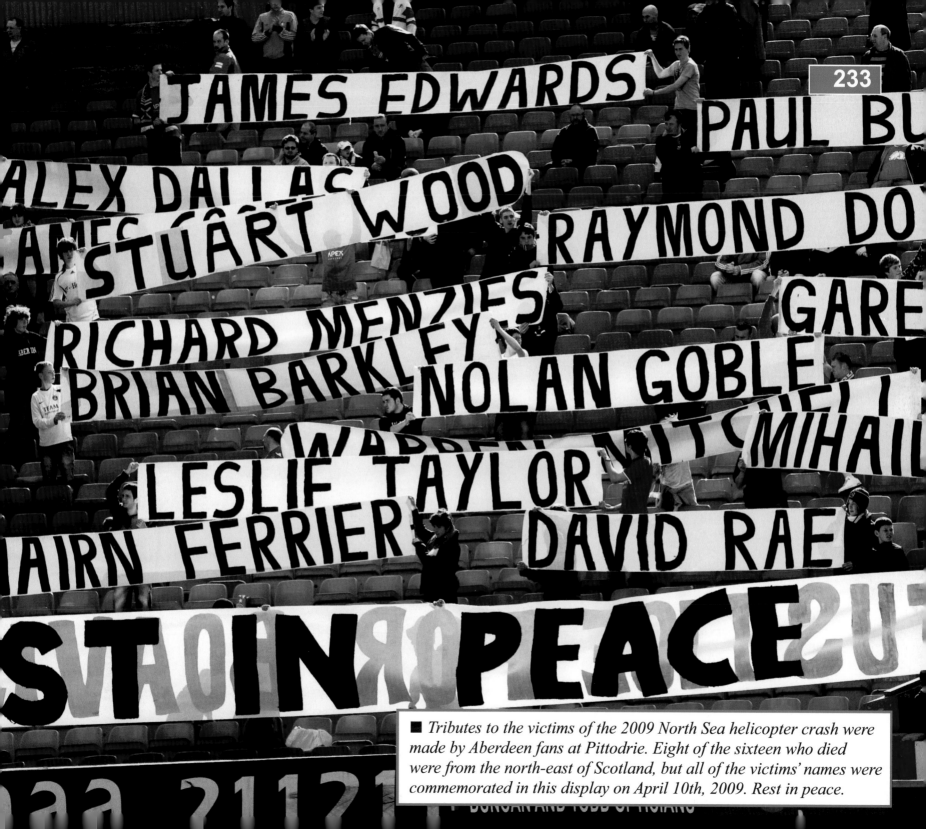

■ *Tributes to the victims of the 2009 North Sea helicopter crash were made by Aberdeen fans at Pittodrie. Eight of the sixteen who died were from the north-east of Scotland, but all of the victims' names were commemorated in this display on April 10th, 2009. Rest in peace.*

■ *The Red Army displays a banner for Remembrance Day in 2014, before a match against Celtic at Pittodrie.*

Angela and Robin Smith had a Dons theme when they married at Pittodrie in June 2017. All seven bridesmaids were in red, and the men wore Aberdeen FC tartan. All the best Angela and Robin.

■ *Fowk do things for the rest of the family, without hope of reward and often with precious little thanks. Let's hear it for the guys who give up their time to plan and set out the pre-match displays. Unsung Red heroes.*

■ *Caring for the Red Family is a tradition that comes from the very top. When Fergie won the Scottish Cup in 1982 the great man celebrated with 13-year-old Joan Taylor, of Middleton Park, who was in a wheelchair at the final.*

■ *The Red Family recognises its heroes. Russell Anderson is an Aberdeen loon, born and bred. He made no secret of his regard for the club, and became the sixth Aberdeen captain to lift silverware when winning the 2014 League Cup. When he retired in 2015, The Red Army stood to recognise a trophy-winning season and the contributions of one of their own.*

Victory parades

I T'S an affy fine sight to see a victorious Dons team parade their latest piece of silverware down Union Street, with all the regiments of the Red Army turned out in force.

Aberdeen is one of the biggest one-club cities in the UK, so the whole town celebrates. The songs bounce back off the granite, voices lifted in triumph. It is always a colourful, happy occasion that brings the streets to a standstill.

Everyone, loyal supporter or not, becomes a fan. They are great days.

■ *This shot is of the 1970 Scottish Cup-winning team on their bus inching its way past the old ABC cinema.*

■ *The arrangements for the 1947 Scottish Cup-winning homecoming are familiar, and yet very much of their time.*

Reports of the day said: "After a vociferous reception on their return to Aberdeen last night with the Scottish Cup, Pittodrie's history-making players were entertained at dinner by the club directors in the Caledonian Hotel.

"Despite torrential rain, many thousands gathered at the Joint Station and along the route to the hotel. There was tremendous enthusiasm as the bus with the players on the roof and captain Frank Dunlop holding the cup aloft, was driven slowly along Guild Street, Regent Quay, Marischal Street and Union Street to Union Terrace.

"After dinner, officials, players and friends were the guests of Mr James Donald at His Majesty's Theatre."

■ *The 2014 League Cup parade was slick and stage-managed...*

but the 1976 League Cup parade was just as much fun.

■ *The 1979-80 League Championship was Aberdeen's first in a quarter of a century. It was also the first time the title had been prised from the Old Firm's greedy grasp since Kilmarnock in 1965. Aberdeen became Scotland's capital city of football success and the Dandies gathered at Pittodrie to pay tribute.*

249

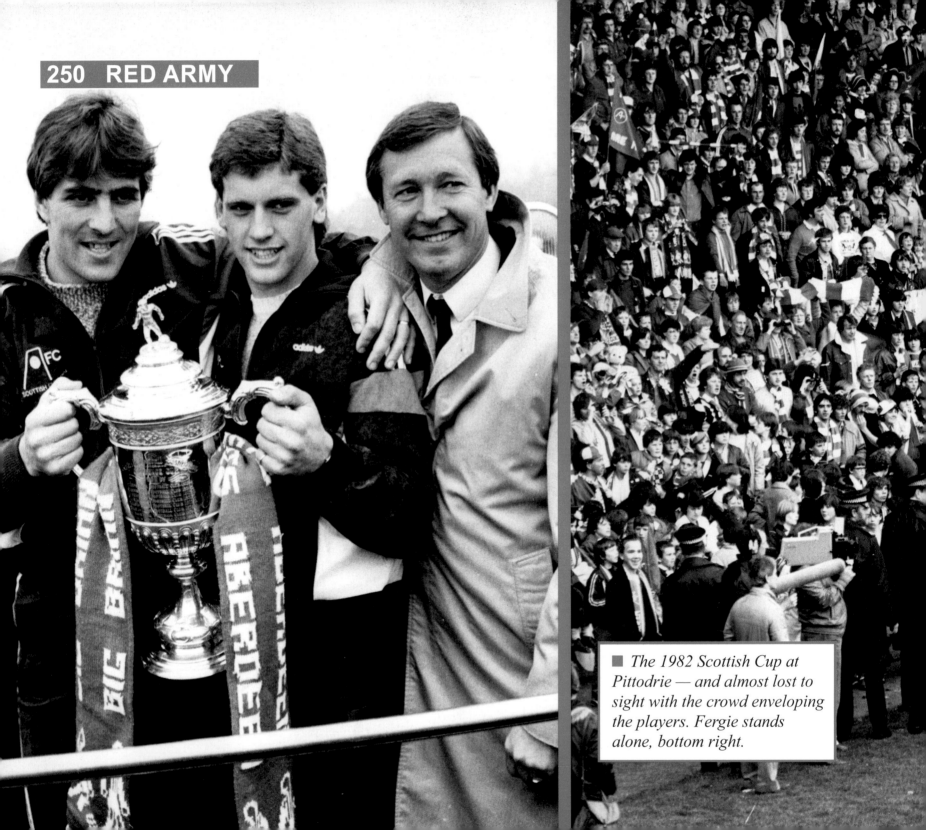

■ *The 1982 Scottish Cup at Pittodrie — and almost lost to sight with the crowd enveloping the players. Fergie stands alone, bottom right.*

■ *Spot the difference. Two photos 13 years apart — Scottish Cup 1970, Scottish and European Cup Winners' Cups 1983.*

253

■ *Aberdeen Trades Club kick up for the celebrations in 1983.*

THE DON'S ARE THE GREATEST.
WINNERS OF
EUROPEAN CUP WINNERS CUP 1983
ALSO SCOTTISH CUP WINNERS 1983

Northern
SCOTTISH

■ *The 1983 procession made its way to Pittodrie after the journey through town, and it felt like this was the real homecoming. The Scottish Cup was one thing, a great thing, but here was a European trophy that had spent the previous year residing in Barcelona, and had been won at the expense of Real Madrid. It had found a new home. It belonged here, Aberdeen Football Club, Pittodrie Street, AB24 5QH.*

By 1984, having the Scottish Cup in town started to feel like the normal state of affairs. And there was a big hand for Alex McLeish.

EUROPEAN CUP WINNERS CUP
WINNERS CUP
ABERDEEN 2 v 1 REAL MADRID

MAGNIFICENT ABERDEEN
DOUBLE CUP
WINNERS

SCOTT
ABERDEE

ABERDEE

ARE MAGIC

ABERDEE

STARS

■ *A crowd of Dons fans at Castle Street cheer the 1986 Scottish Cup winners.*

And glasses were raised in their honour outside the Malt Mill.

■ *1986. The fourth glorious Scottish Cup win in five years. Those were the days my friends, we thought they'd never end.*

■ *2014. And, of course, the glory days didn't end and won't end.*

Aberdeen FC is a forward-thinking, ambitious and highly-professional club. It is a club that will win trophies in the future, lots of trophies.

It is merely a matter of time.

The wait between Hampden victories or successful league championships feels long and is often frustrating. But football has always existed on a great big wheel. Sometimes you are up, sometimes the wheel turns and you are down.

You keep supporting your club, though. It never leaves you.

The celebration days are the reward for keeping the faith.

Colours that just don't run

THERE is a tribalism to football that sets it apart from any other sport on the planet. A football fan is passionate, committed, loud and proud, and any book that is about supporters has to acknowledge this part of the experience.

But a real fan is not violent, because only idiots lose control of themselves to such an extent. But you aggressively support The Dons. If the opposition sing, then you drown them out. If they think they've got witty observations to make in song or with banners, then you outdo them, fire right back at them, or even provoke them.

The Dons fans have several rivals. There is the so-called "New Firm" arguments with Dundee United. Then there's the North Derby that geographically claims Inverness Caley Thistle and Ross County as rivals for the Red Army. And there might soon be a city-based challenge if Cove's rise takes them into the top league.

But the real aggravation is reserved for Rangers.

Various incidents and injustices over the years have fuelled this rivalry, and there have been some unsavoury aspects (with fault on both sides). But it should be noted that there is no sectarian element to the antipathy. It's good to beat them though.

■ *Jibes over the Rangers-Aberdeen divide at Pittodrie in September 2016. The Dons won 2-1.*

GIVE WAY
50 yds

269

Aberdeen casuals escorted through Dundee for a Scottish Cup Quarter-Final at Dens Park in March 1986.

■ *Mounted police were needed for this band of casuals after The Dons trounced Rangers 3-0 at Ibrox in September 1985.*

271

The modern treatment of Dons fans in Glasgow is still hostile.

■ *There is no prejudice. The Red Army holds Rangers and Celtic fans in equal regard.*

■ *The old Beach End in full voice.*

276   RED ARMY

■ *Left. Whoever the opposition, wherever you are — Stand Free.*

Dunfermline away, in the Scottish Cup 2009.

■ *Right — There are times when partisan support goes off the rails. This photo is from an Aberdeen-Celtic match at Pittodrie on October 28, 1972.*

The early 1970s saw an explosion of violence on football terraces around the UK.

This 16-year-old girl, a school pupil, was carried from the crowd with a knife sticking from her head. She was, thankfully, allowed home from hospital that evening after receiving treatment.

To throw a knife in a crowd is the work of an idiot.

Fans support their teams with passion, but taking a knife to a match is the act of a coward. All true football fans will condemn and despise such behaviour.

This isn't, and never was, what being a football fan is about.

The Scottish Cup Semi-Final 2012. A 2-1 loss to Hibs.

Once a Red...

NO team wins all the time. Good times come around, bad times come around. There are great victories, there are losses that leave you shaking your head, asking: "How did that happen?"

Any book that purports to show football fans in their natural environment has to include the dirges of defeat as well as the songs of glory.

No matter what happens on the field, you support your team.

No matter that it is biting cold, with a cutting wind, the skies are chucking down sleet, and you're standing on some godforsaken ancient terracing with no roof, miserable to the core, you support your team.

Whichever players are wearing the shirts, you support your team. If it's all going wrong and the opposition fans are dancing with glee, you support your team. When all else in life fails you, you support your team

Come hell or high water, you support your team.

Even when you feel like you can't take any more, you support your team — The Dons.

Always a Red

■ *The Scottish Cup Quarter-Final replay 2008. Put out on penalties by lower-league Dunfermline.*

■ *A Europa League Qualifier in 2009.*
Mark McGhee's first competivive match
at Pittodrie. It was a 5-1 defeat to
Sigma Olomouc of the Czech Republic.

The Scottish Cup Final 2017. A 2-1 loss to Celtic.

■ *The last home game of a dismal season, 2003-04. The Dons finished second bottom of the Premier League, and lost this game 2-1 to Dundee. Yes, Dundee! But still The Red Army turned out in good numbers.*

■ *The 2012 Scottish Cup Semi-Final loss to Hibernian was another tough one to take. The Dons were well above Hibs in the league and at stake was a place in the final against Hearts. It was a decent chance to bring home silverware. But Leigh Griffiths scored a late winner for the Edinburgh team. Another missed opportunity.*

■ *It is with a heavy heart that we come to the worst of them all. THAT Scottish Cup Semi-Final of 2008 against Queen of the South at Hampden. The Red Army started the game in fine spirits . . .*

But it went horribly and painfully wrong. It had all looked so promising after Jimmy Calderwood's Dons had recorded a fine win at Celtic Park in the quarters.

■ *Somehow the disappointment of young fans feels particularly bad. League Cup Final 2016.*

■ *Scottish Cup Final 2017.*

■ *League Cup Semi-Final 2011.*

■ *Scottish Cup Semi-Final 2012.*

■ *But it is important that you keep the faith because there will always be glories to come, and winning feels so very, very good.*

A sense of humour

Quine Victoria gets ready for the 2017 Scottish Cup Final.

SOMETIMES, when you're the type of person who goes to the fitba, you have to laugh. Because if you didn't laugh, you'd cry! What are those half-hearted, excuses for footballers doing in my team's colours?

But, quite apart from comedy defending and laughter-inducing attempts at finishing, you also need to be able to take a joke and fire a joke back. You need to be a little tolerant, able to laugh at yourself — you should not, under any circumstances, have a thin skin.

So to end this book, hopefully we can raise a smile.

Some of what is termed "humour" in this chapter is just daft antics. There are a couple of jokes with a jag . . . and some people deserve all they get!

291

■ *December 21st, 1996. Five Reds get in the festive mood. Unfortunately, the Dons defence also put on a Santa act, gifting Killie three goals at Rugby Park. Ho. Ho. Oh no.*

■ *The Red Army has always excelled in the art of the provocative banner. This was at Tannadice on January 1st, 2014.*

SINCE 1903

■ *The Dandies tend to save the sharpest side of their wit for Rangers supporters. But Glasgow folk, famously, all have a great sense of humour don't they? The blue-clad comedy fans must have loved these banter banners.*

2017 Scottish Cup Final. If you're going to wear one of these skin-tight suits, then strategic bum-bag placement is essential.

■ *Scottish Cup Semis 2011. These lads had been feeling cocky about the result, but it was a limp performance in the end. Still, it's never as big a thing as you think it is lads, no matter what you tell everyone.*

THE RED ARMY ★★

CELEBRATING DONS SUPPORTERS

MANY people work on putting together a book like this. Information is gathered from various sources and there are all sorts of logistical problems to be considered and overcome. I am humbly grateful for the time, expertise, good ideas, and downright cleverness that I have encountered.

Those who deserve medals for valour in setting **The Red Army** to march include:

Gary Thomas, Kirsty Smith, David Powell, Barry Sullivan and Duncan Laird for photo-scanning, metadata management and archive wizardry. Research is always the most time-consuming job.

Stewart Alexander, for his deep Aberdeen FC knowledge and the generous gift of photos to fill in gaps I had no other way of filling. Also Grant Millar, an old, old friend, who introduced me to Stewart.

The office team who do things concerning book economics, printing and production that I do not even pretend to understand: Sylwia Jackowska, Jacqui Hunter, James Kirk, Paula Gibson, Susan Heron, Gill Martin, and Craig Houston.

Richard Gordon for a heartfelt and insightful foreword. A true Don.

Artists Gary Aitchison, Leon Strachan and Mark McIlmail, who created what I think is a highly impressive book cover.

Steve Flight, Kelly Davidson and Lynn Connor who know all sorts of clever things about advertising.

Louise Anderson, Liesa Black, and Rona Rodriguez who persuade people to buy this book.

Sheena Nicoll for her Doric pronunciation expertise.

Emily Tsang for marketing advice.

And for various reasons: Bill & Chris Nicoll, Carole Finan, Lewis & Rebecca Finan, Alison Duncan, Craig Bertie, Pip Gerrard, Maggie Dun, and Fraser T. Ogilvie

And last but certainly not least, our sponsors and partners Muehlhan, who are fitba people and supporters of Aberdeen FC and the Granite City.

Steve Finan, 2019.

If you liked this book, you'll love these two

Lifted Over The Turnstiles and *It's A Team Game*

Scottish Football Grounds In The Black & White Era   *Scottish Football Club Line-Ups In The Black & White Era*

Scottish football nostalgia from the point of view of fans — not players
who will move on to other clubs; managers who are there to be blamed; or
journalists who have their own agenda; but the people who went to watch
fitba in the black & white era because they truly loved the game.

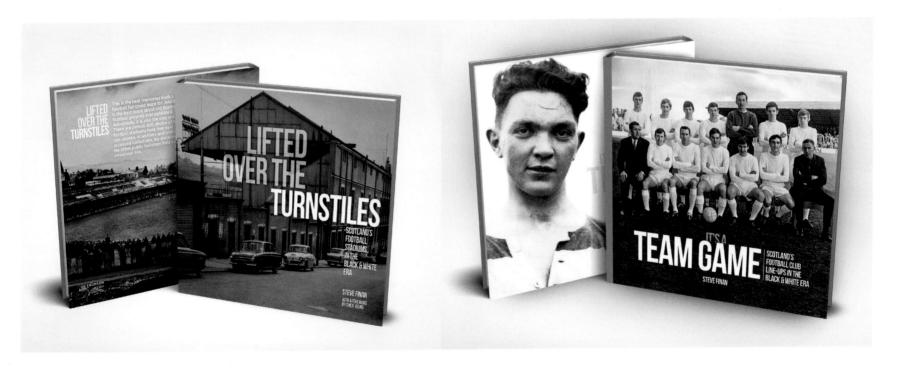